Könemann Study Scores

Johannes Brahms

Sämtliche Klavierwerke
Complete Piano Works
Œuvres complètes pour piano

Urtext

*

Sonaten, Variationen, 51 Übungen
Klavierstücke · Piano Pieces · Morceaux pour piano
(Scherzo, Balladen, Rhapsodien, Tänze, Fantasien, Intermezzi, Klavierstücke, 5 Studien)

*

Herausgegeben von · Edited by · Edité par
Enikő Gyenge

Study Score Edition

KM 4012

Könemann Music Budapest

Johannes Brahms
(1833–1897)

Sonaten, Variationen, 51 Übungen

K 114 & 115 & 191
Könemann Music Budapest

INDEX

Sonaten

Sonate in C Op. 1

pag.

6

Sonate in fis Op. 2

40

Sonate in f Op. 5

70

Variationen

Variationen in fis
über ein Thema von Robert Schumann Op. 9

106

Variationen in D
über ein eigenes Thema Op. 21, No. 1

Thema

126

Variationen in D
über ein ungarisches Lied Op. 21, No. 2

138

Variationen und Fuge in B
über ein Thema von Händel Op. 24

148

Variationen in a
über ein Thema von Paganini Op. 35/I

Thema

174

Variationen in a
über ein Thema von Paganini Op. 35/II

Thema

191

51 Übungen

208

Appendix

Thema mit Variationen
Op. 18/II

284

Sonaten

Joseph Joachim zugeeignet

Sonate in C

Op. 1
Hamburg, 1852-53

Andante

(Nach einem altdeutschen Minneliede)

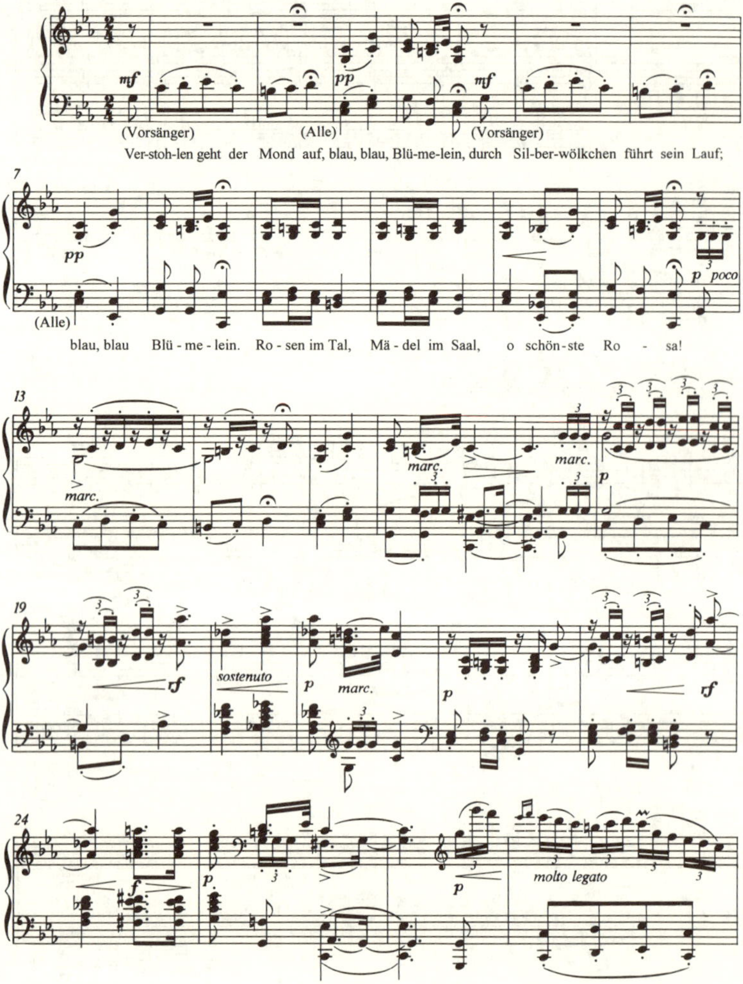
(Vorsänger)
(Alle)
(Vorsänger)
Ver-stoh-len geht der Mond auf, blau, blau, Blü-me-lein, durch Sil-ber-wölkchen führt sein Lauf;
(Alle)
blau, blau Blü - me - lein. Ro - sen im Tal, Mä - del im Saal, o schön-ste Ro - sa!
poco
marc.
marc.
marc.
sostenuto
marc.
molto legato

 K 114

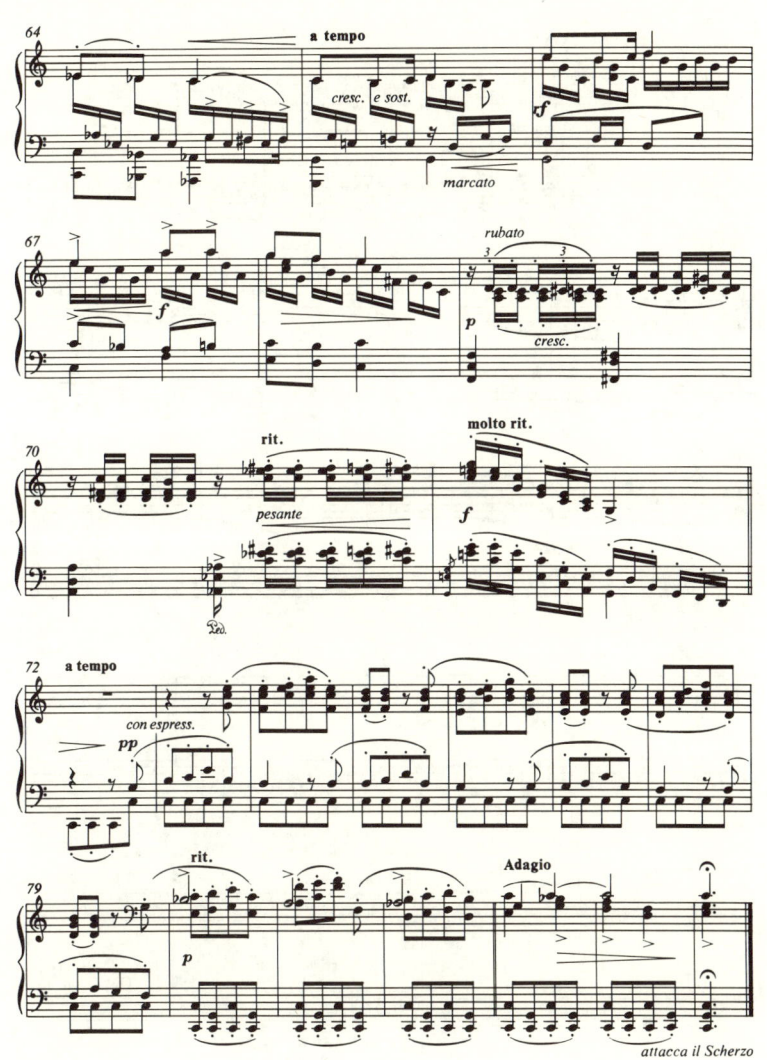

Scherzo
Allegro molto e con fuoco

*) Die kleine Noten können nötigenfalls wegbleiben (Brahms).

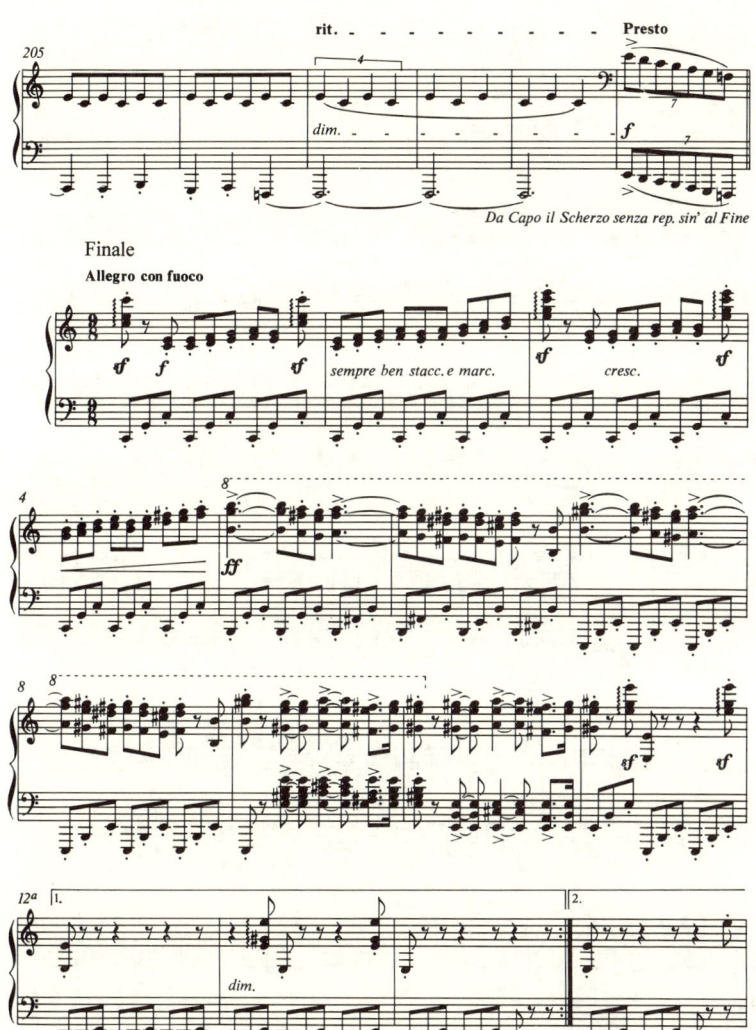

Frau Clara Schumann verehrend zugeeignet
Sonate in fis

Op. 2
Hamburg, 1854

Frau Gräfin von Hohenthal gewidmet
Sonate in f

Op. 5
Düsseldorf, 1853

*) Die kleine Noten können nötigenfalls wegbleiben (Brahms).

"Der abend Dämmert, das Mondlicht scheint,
Da sind zwei Herzen in Liebe vereint
Und halten sich selig umfangen."

Sternau

Andante

Scherzo

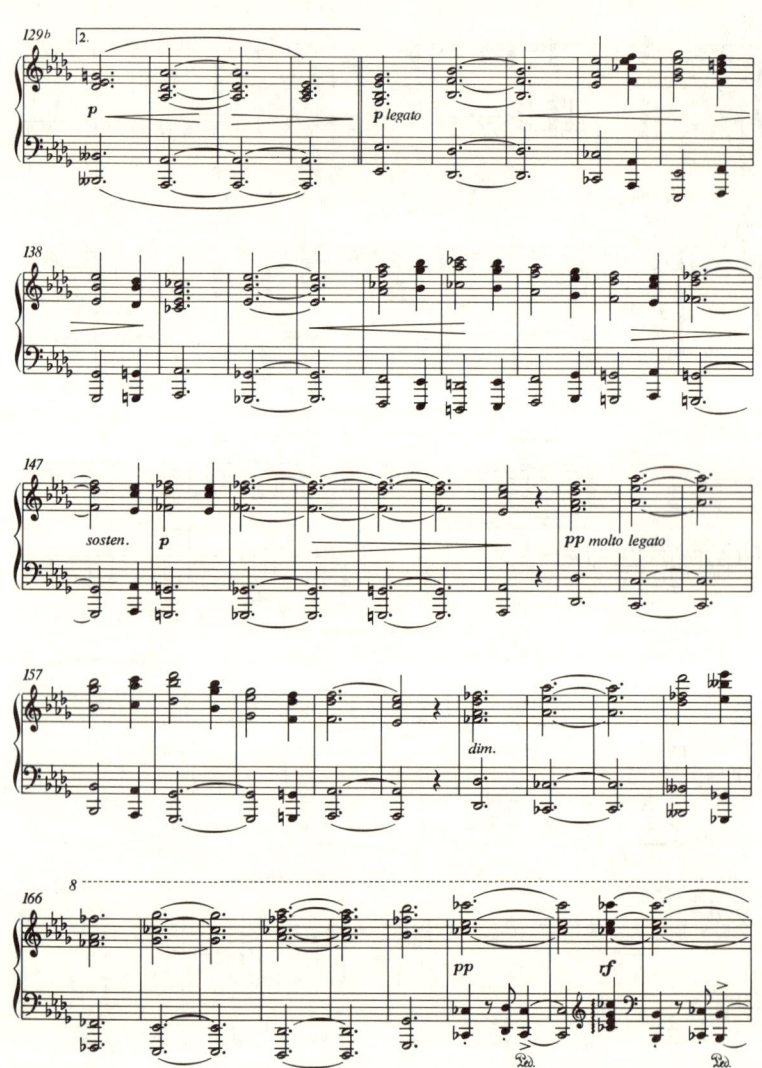

Intermezzo
(Rückblick)

Finale

Variationen

Frau Clara Schumann zugeeignet

Variationen in fis
über ein Thema von Robert Schumann

Op. 9
Düsseldorf, 1854

Var. VI
Allegro

Var. XIV
Andante

Var. XV
Poco Adagio
espressivo

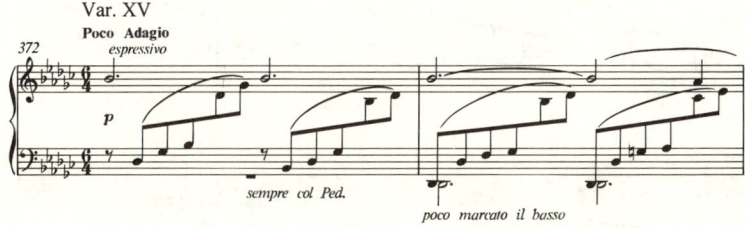

sempre col Ped.

poco marcato il basso

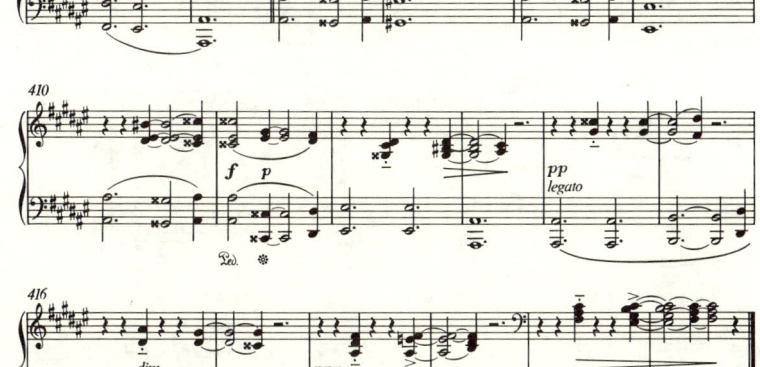

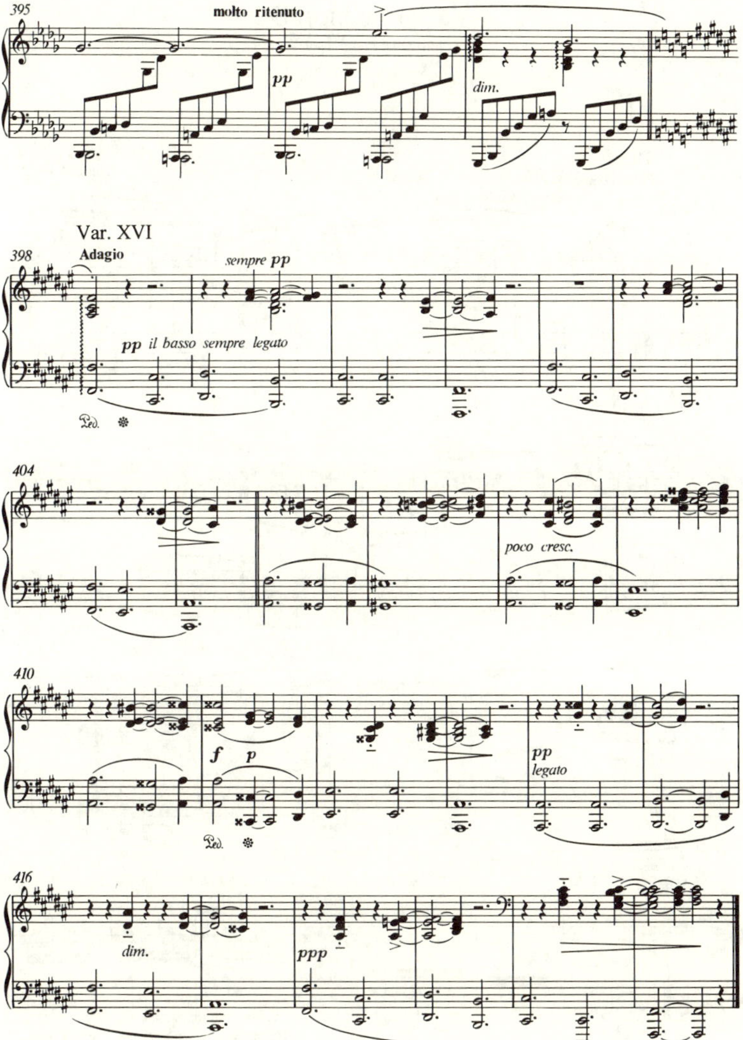
395
molto ritenuto
pp
dim.
Var. XVI
398
Adagio
sempre pp
pp il basso sempre legato
Ped.
404
poco cresc.
410
f
p
Ped.
pp
legato
416
dim.
ppp

Var. V
Tempo di tema

Var. VI
Più moto
espressivo

p legato

Più facile

Var. VIII
Allegro non troppo

Variationen in D
über ein ungarisches Lied

Op. 21, No. 2

Variationen und Fuge in B

über ein Thema von Händel

Op. 24
Hamburg, 1861

Variationen in a
über ein Thema von Paganini

Thema

"Studien für Pianoforte", Op. 35/I
Wien, 1862-63

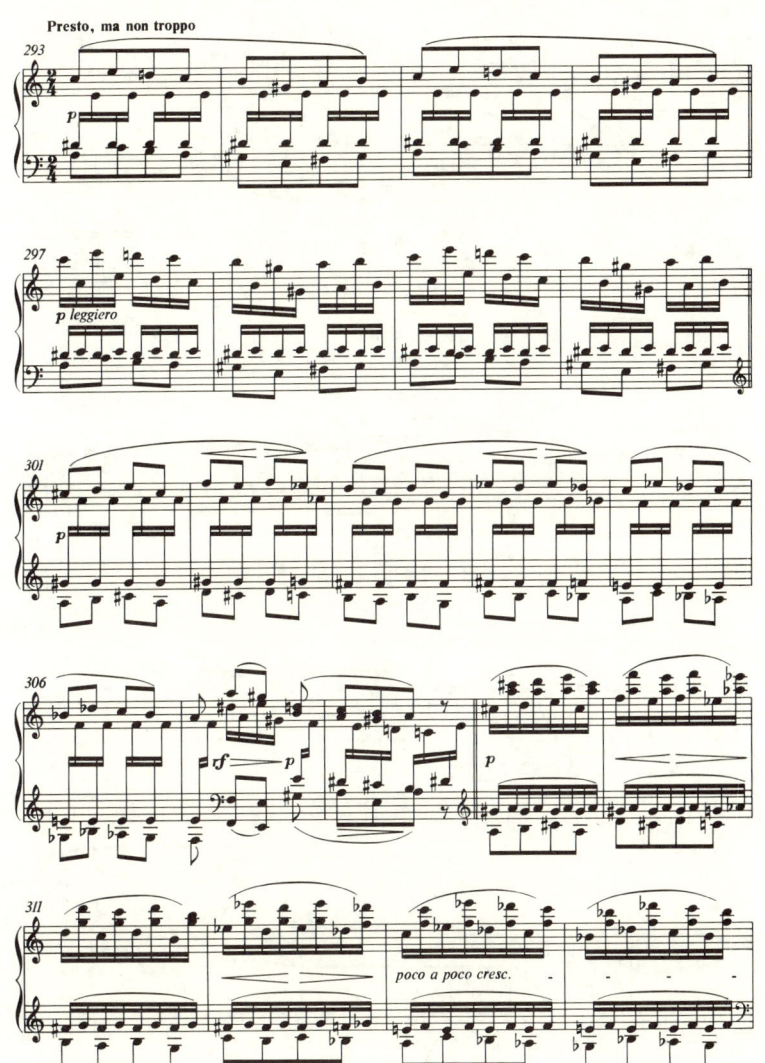

Variationen in a
über ein Thema von Paganini

"Studien für Pianoforte", Op. 35/II

Var. X
Feroce, energico

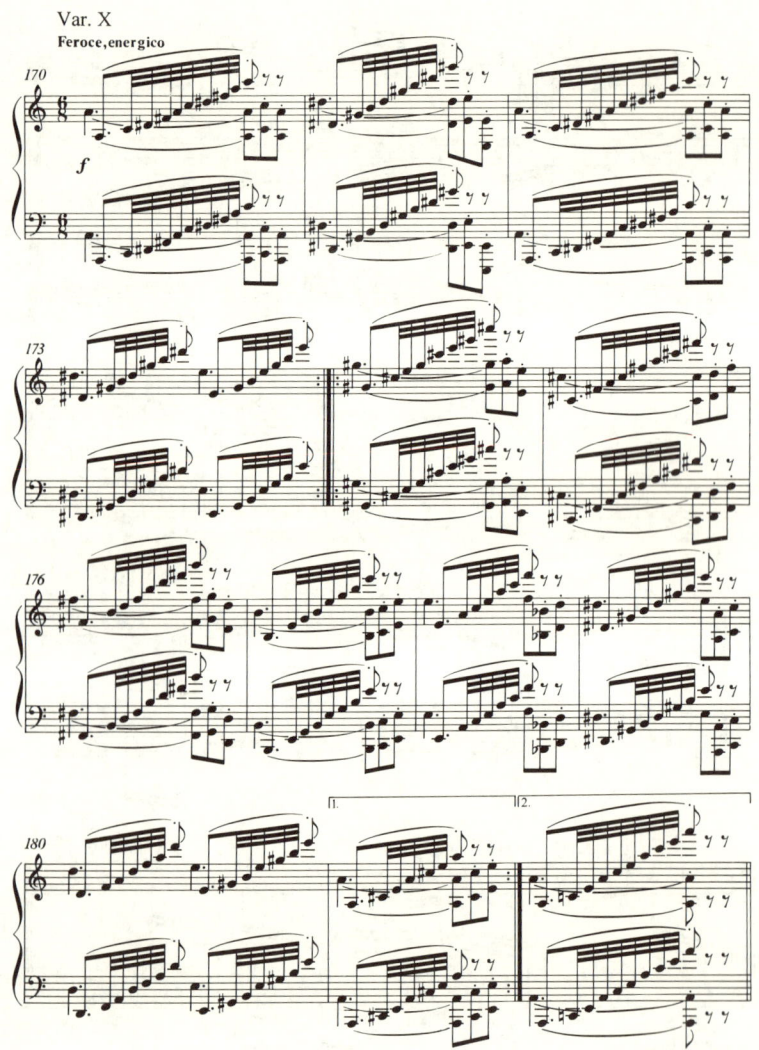

51 Übungen

51 Übungen für Pianoforte

WoO 6

* Diese und änliche Übungen auch in anderen Tonarten zu üben. (Etwa 1b in A-Dur, 1c E-Dur und so fort.) Abwechslung im Zeitmaß und Tonstärke bleiben dem Spieler überlassen.

These similar exercises are to be played in other keys. (Probably 1b in A major, 1c in E major and so on.) Changes of tempo and dynamics are left to the player's discretion.

Ces exercices, ainsi que les semblables, doivent être joués aussi dans d'autres tons (probablement 1b en la majeur, 1c en mi majeur, et ainsi de suite). Des changements quant au tempo et dynamique sont laissés à la guise du joueur.

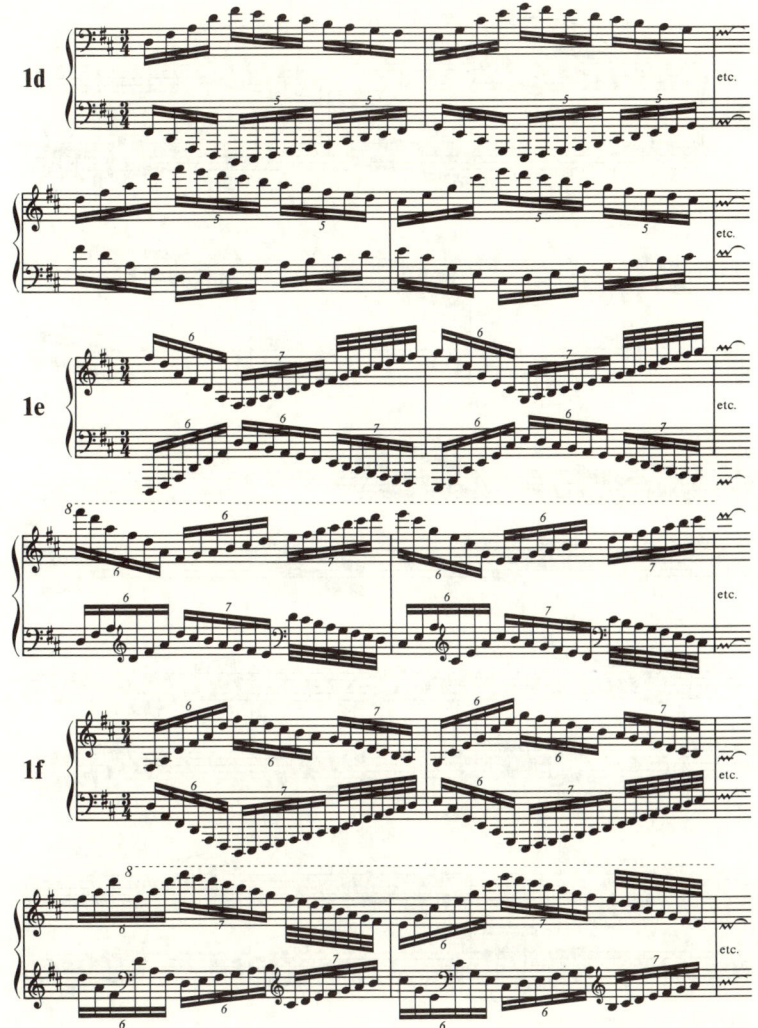

* Nach Belieben in weiteren Oktaven.
  Ad lib. in further octaves.
  Ad libitum sur d'autres octaves.

* Wie oben.
 As before.
 Comme précédemment.

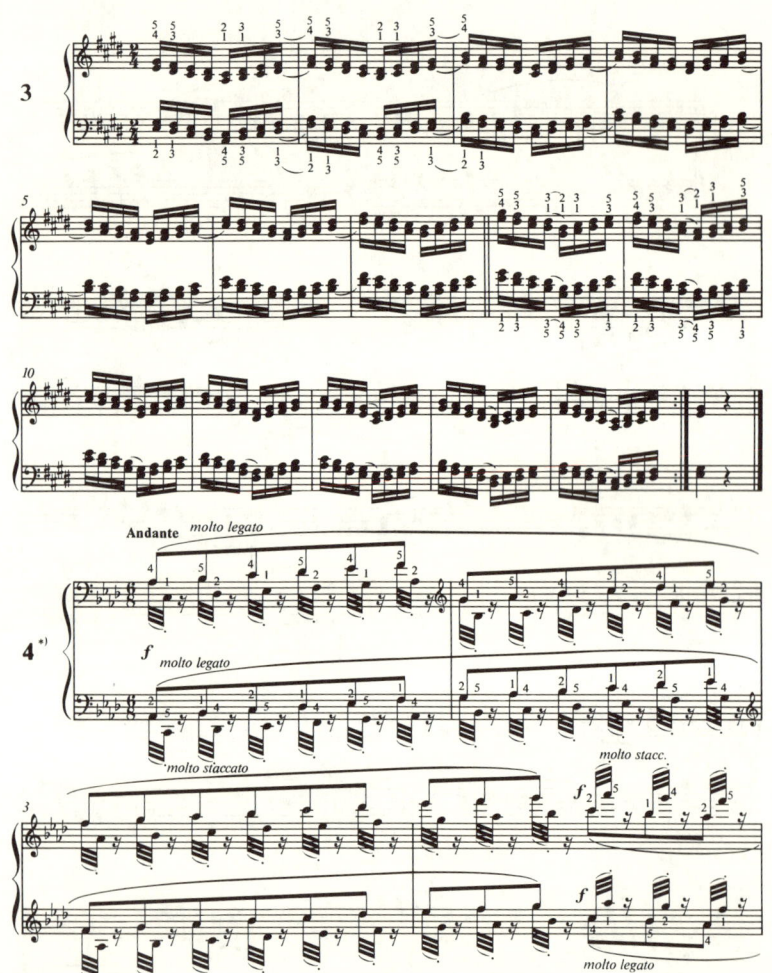

* Vorübung für Tonleitern in Sexten, bei denen durchaus (wie in Terzen-Tonleitern) aufwärts die obern Töne, abwärts die untern zu binden sind.

Preparatory exercise for scales for sixths where upwards the upper notes, downwards the lower notes should be slurred throughout (as in scales in thirds).

Exercice préparatoire aux gammes en sextes, où, comme dans les gammes de tierces, en montant ce sont les notes d'en haut, en descendent ce sont les notes d'en bas qui doivent être liées.

* Kleine Wiederholungen (:|:) innerhalb einer Übung: ad lib.
  Short repeats (:|:) within an exercise ad lib.
  Petites reprises (:|:) dans un exercice même ad lib.

* Vorübung zu Nr. 5.
  Preparatory exercise to No. 5.
  Exercice préparatoire au N° 5.

* Vorübung zu Nr. 6.
 Preparatory exercise to No. 6.
 Exercice préparatoire au N° 6.

* Die Wiederholungen (:‖:) eine und zwei Oktaven höher oder tiefer.
  The repeats (:‖:) one and two octaves higher or lower.
  Les reprises (:‖:) une ou deux octaves plus haut ou plus bas.

* Die Wiederholungen (:||:) eine und zwei Oktaven höher oder tiefer.
  The repeats (:||:) one and two octaves higher or lower.
  Les reprises (:||:) une ou deux octaves plus haut ou plus bas.

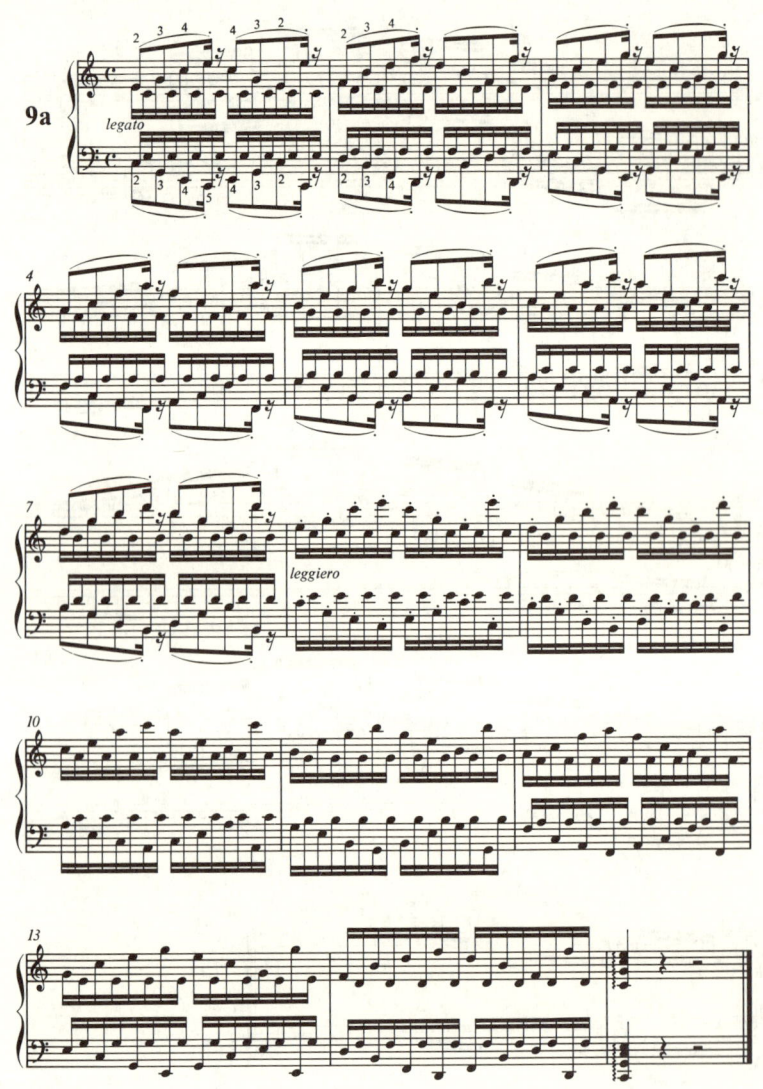

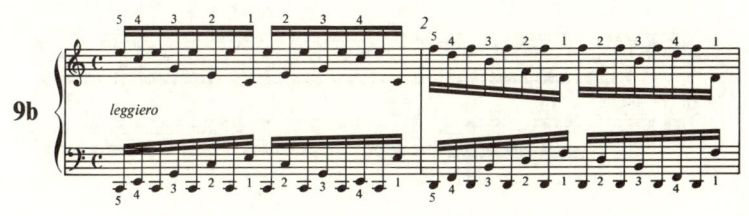

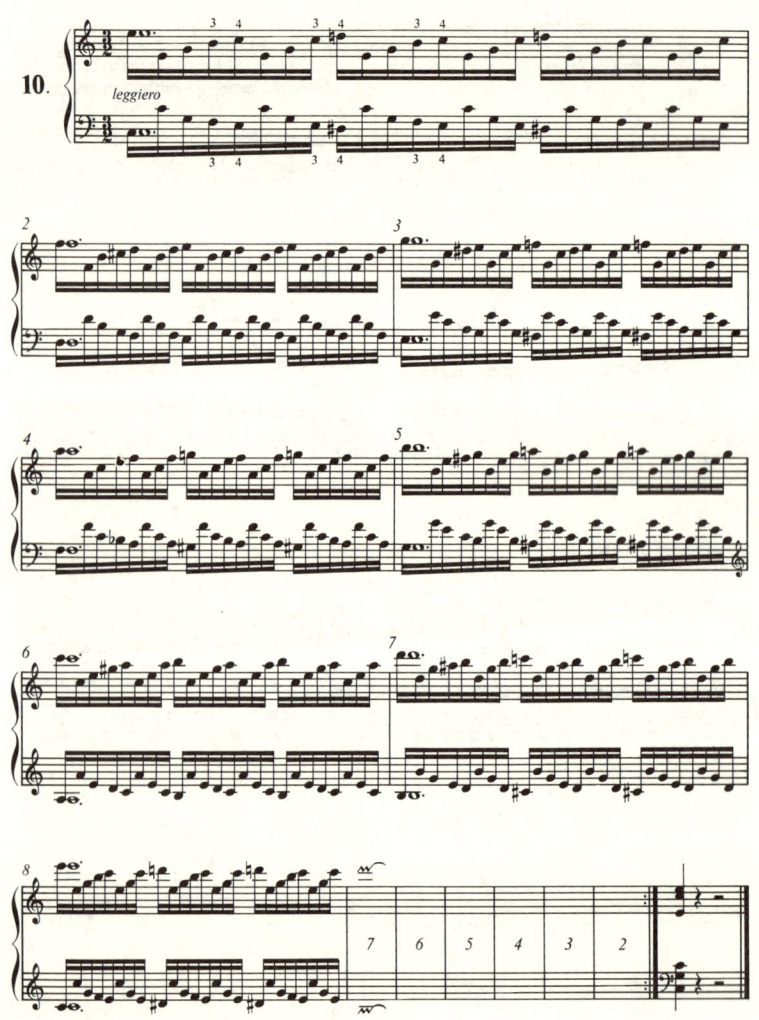

15.

16a

* Die eingeklammerten Noten (O) werden nicht angeschlagen, sondern nur während der Übung ausgehalten.
  Notes in brackets (O) should be held down silently during the whole exercise.
  Les notes entre paranthèses (O) doivent être des notes soutenues durant tout l'exercice, sans être frappées.

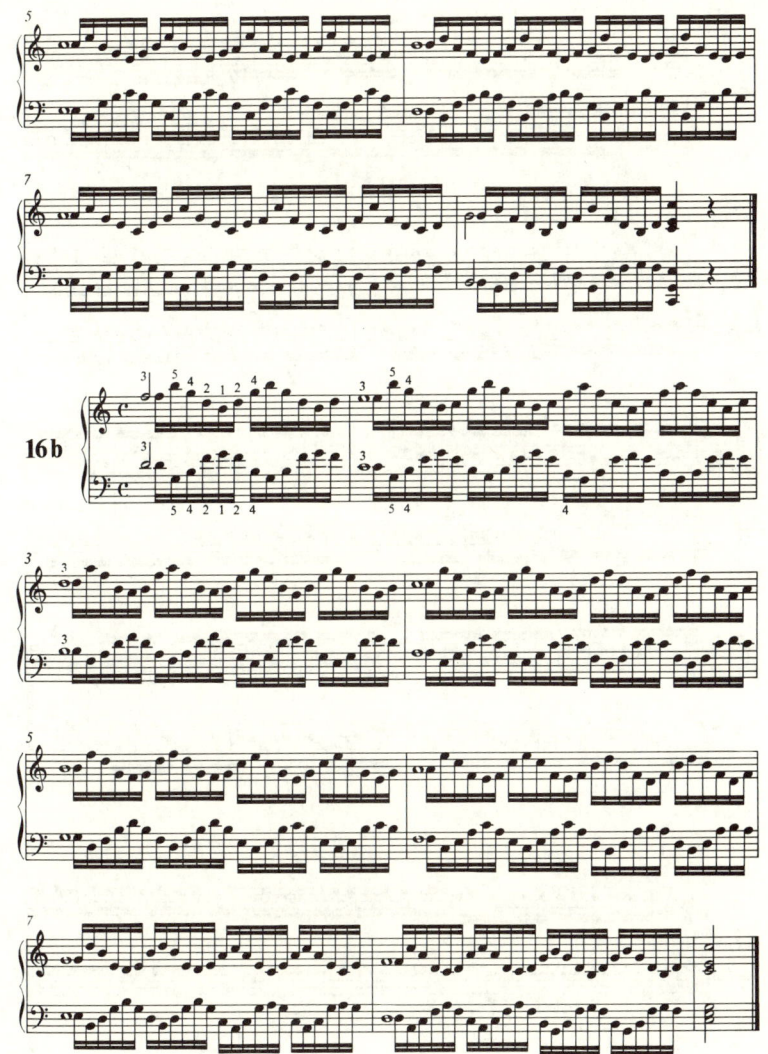

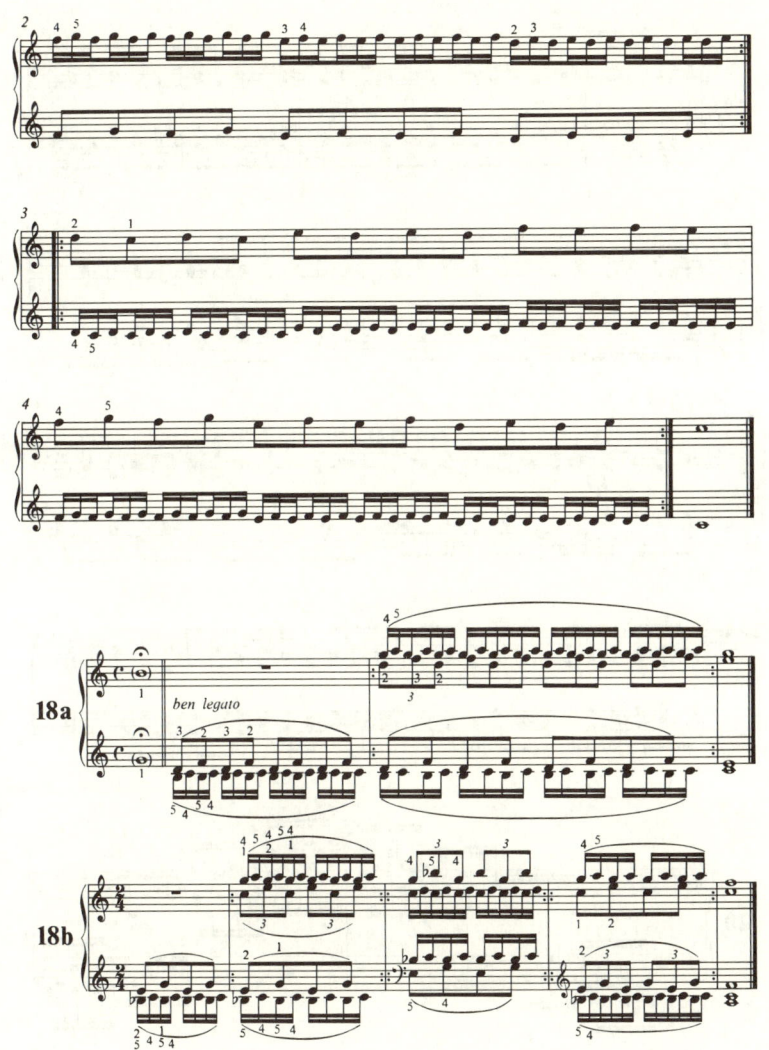

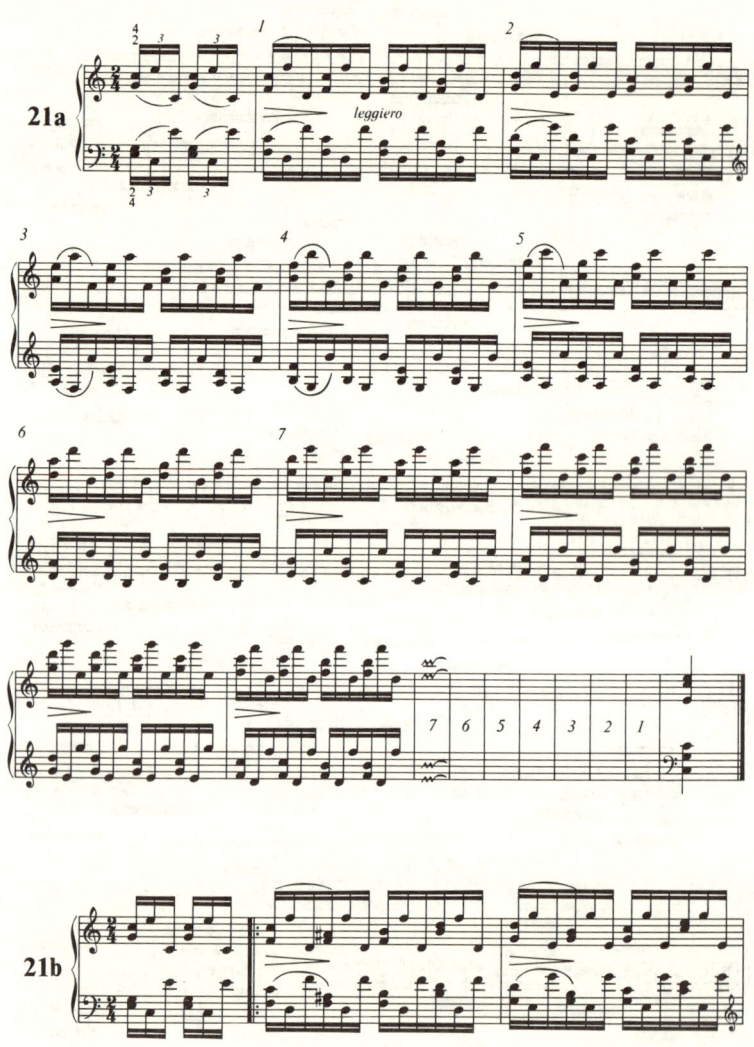

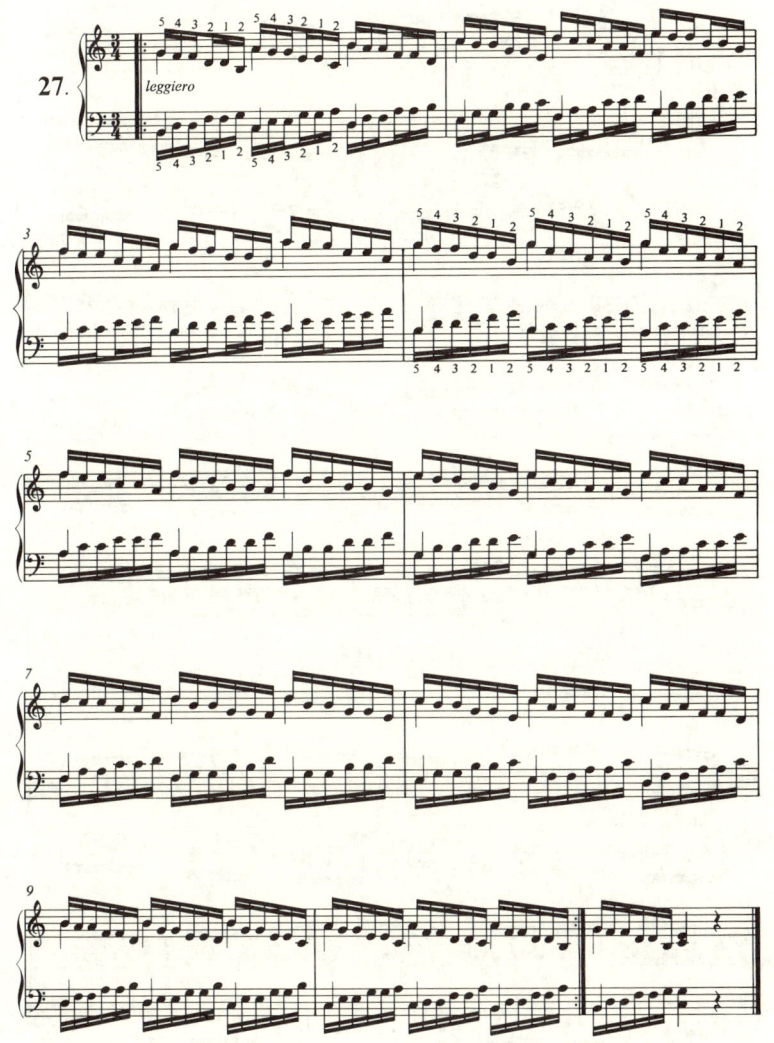

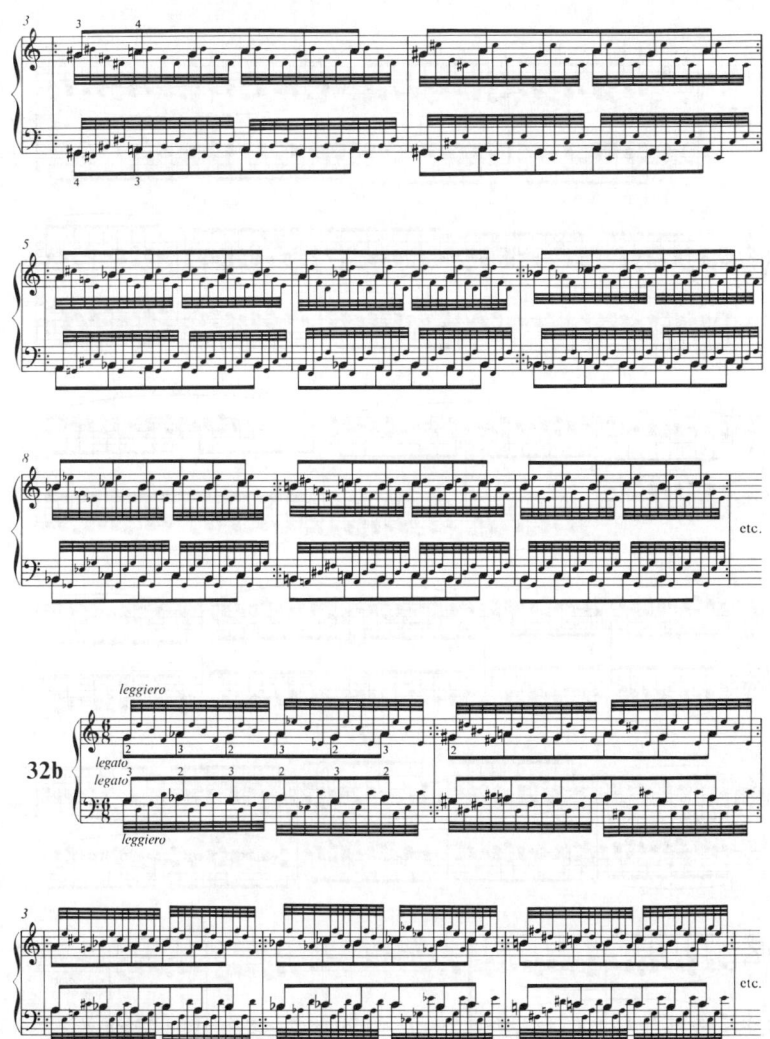

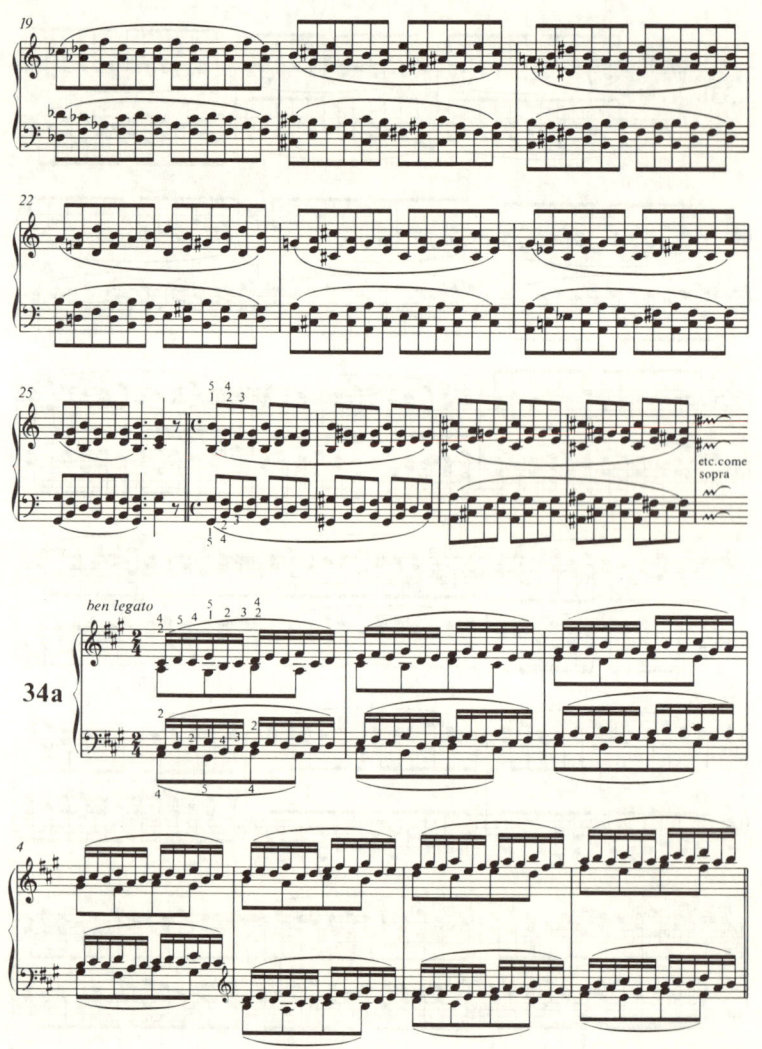

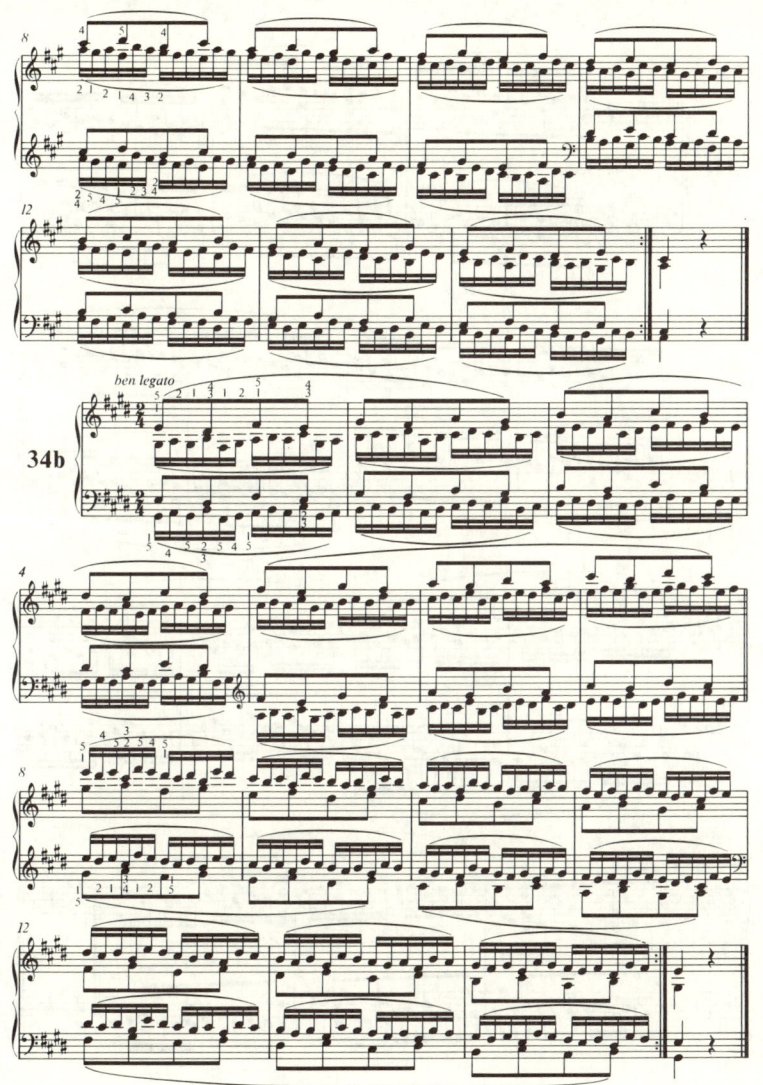

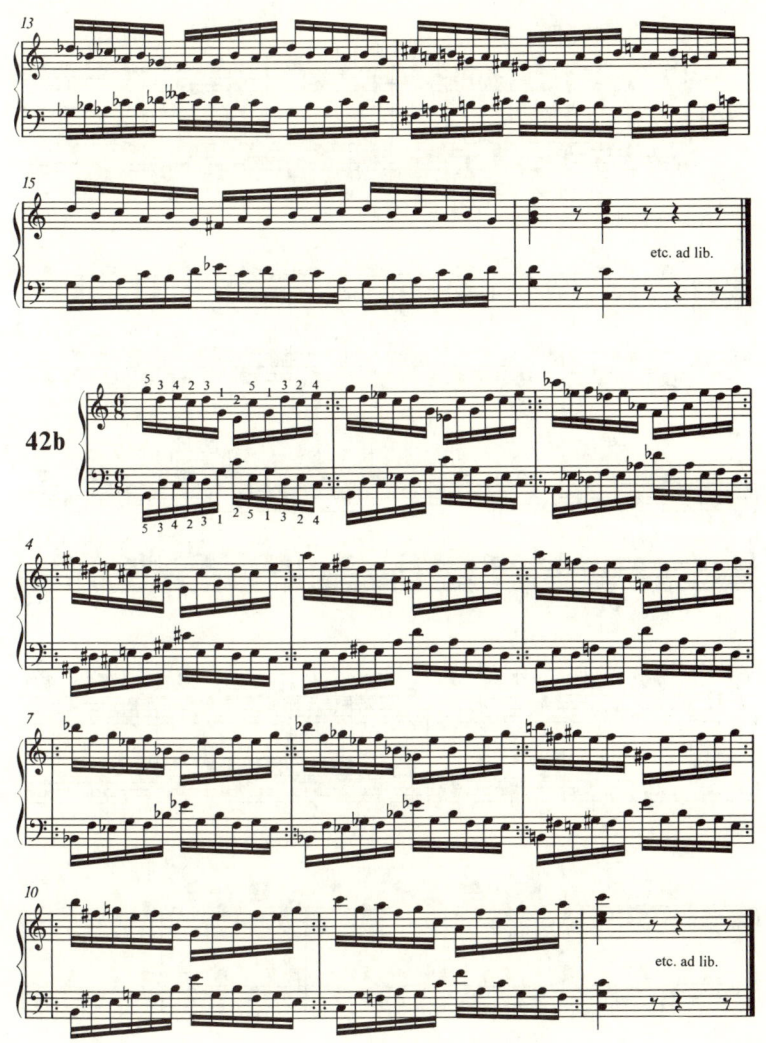

etc. simile come sopra

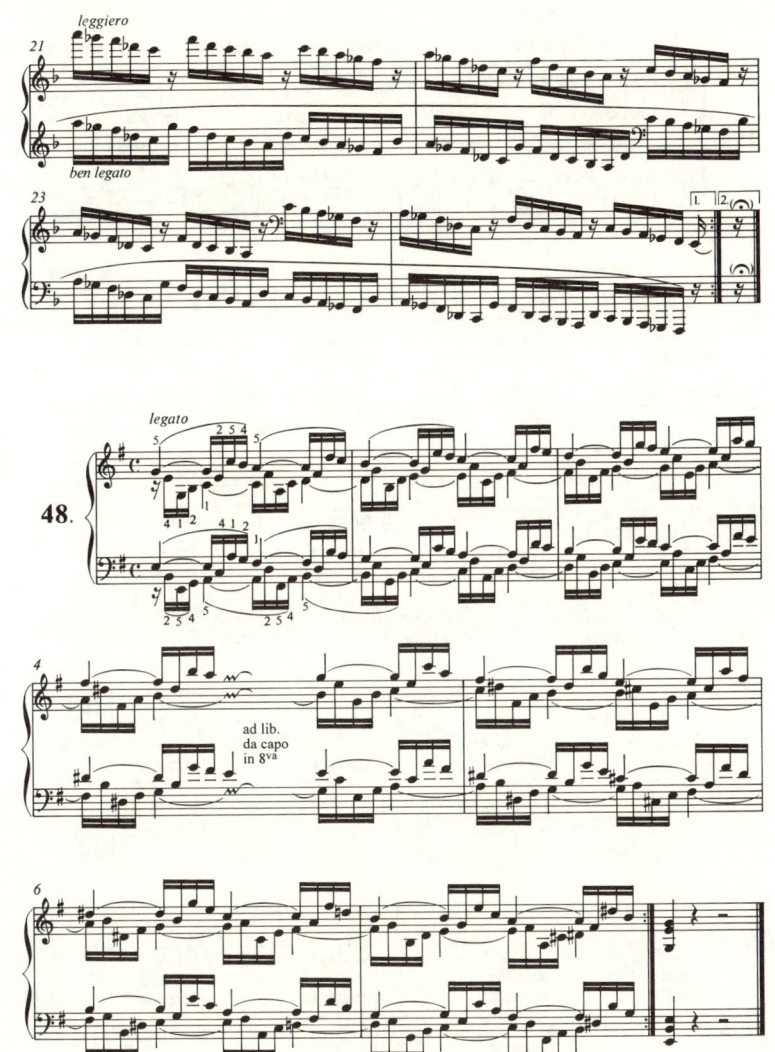

APPENDIX

Clara Schumann zugeeignet
Zum 13. September 1860 als freundlichen Gruß

Thema mit Variationen

Op. 18/II
Hamburg–Bonn, 1860

KÖNEMANN MUSIC BUDAPEST

URTEXT

TASCHENPARTITUREN
POCKET SCORES

Johann Sebastian Bach

Das wohltemperierte Klavier I–II

Französische Suiten & Englische Suiten

Inventionen, Sinfonien, Kleine Präludien und Fughetten

Klavierübung I–IV
(6 Partiten, Italienisches Konzert, Französische Ouverture, 4 Duette, Goldberg-Variationen)

Ludwig van Beethoven

Piano Complete
(Leinenband im Schuber – *Cloth-bound, slipcase*)

    Kleinere Klavierwerke – *Piano Pieces*
(Rondi, Kleine Sonaten, Sonatinen, Klavierstücke, Bagatelle, Tänze)
Sonaten I–II
Variationen

32 Klaviersonaten in 2 Bänden
(Leinenband im Schuber)
32 Piano Sonatas in 2 volumes
(Cloth-bound, slipcase)

EINZELBÄNDE – *SEPARATE VOLUMES*

Kleinere Klavierwerke – *Piano Pieces*
Variationen

Johannes Brahms

Piano Complete
(Leinenband im Schuber – *Cloth-bound, slipcase*)

    Klavierstücke – *Piano Pieces*
(Scherzo, Balladen, Rhapsodien, Tänze, Fantasien, Intermezzi, Klavierstücke, 5 Studien)
Sonaten, Variationen, 51 Übungen

Joseph Haydn

Piano Complete
(Leinenband im Schuber – *Cloth-bound, slipcase*)

    Klavierstücke – *Piano Pieces*
Sonaten I–II

Wolfgang Amadeus Mozart

Piano Complete
(Leinenband im Schuber – *Cloth-bound, slipcase*)

    Klavierstücke und Variationen
Sonaten, Fantasien und Rondi

GROSSFORMAT
PLAYING SCORES

Carl Philipp Emanuel Bach

Sämtliche Klavierwerke in 14 Bänden
Complete Piano Works *in 14 volumes*
(Leinenband im 3 Schuber – *Cloth-bound in 3 slipcases*)

I 1. Die 6 "Preussischen" Sonaten,
  Die 6 "Württembergischen" Sonaten
 2. 6 Sonatinen, 6 Sonaten mit veränderten Reprisen
 3. 6 Sonaten ("Erste Fortsetzung"),
  6 Sonaten ("Zweite Fortsetzung")
 4. 18 "Probestücke" in 6 Sonaten,
  6 Sonatine nuove, 6 leichte Sonaten,
  6 Sonaten ("Damensonaten")

Ludwig van Beethoven

Piano Complete
(Leinenband im Schuber – *Cloth-bound, slipcase*)

 Klavierstücke und Bagatelle
 Rondi, Kleine Sonaten, Sonatinen
 Sonaten
 Tänze
 Variationen

Sonaten in 3 Bänden
 (Leinenband im Schuber)
Sonatas *in 3 volumes*
 (Cloth-bound, slipcase)

Johannes Brahms

Piano Complete
(Leinenband im Schuber – *Cloth-bound, slipcase*)

Klavierstücke
 Scherzo, Balladen, Rhapsodien, Tänze,
 Fantasien, Intermezzi, Klavierstücke

Sonaten, Variationen

5 Studien, 51 Übungen

Joseph Haydn

Piano Complete
(Leinenband im Schuber – *Cloth-bound, slipcase*)

 Klavierstücke – *Piano Pieces*
 Sonaten I–II–III

Wolfgang Amadeus Mozart

Piano Complete
(Leinenband im Schuber – *Cloth-bound, slipcase*)

 Klavierstücke
 Sonaten, Fantasien und Rondi I–II
 Variationen

Die Bände sind auch einzeln lieferbar.
The volumes are also separately available.

Der Notentext der vorliegenden Taschenpartiturausgabe ist
identisch mit der Urtextausgabe sämtlicher Werke Brahms',
herausgegeben von Könemann Music Budapest im Großformat.
Die Originalausgabe enthält den Kritischen Bericht.

The musical text of the present Study Score Edition is identical with the
Urtext-edition of Brahms' complete piano works published
by Könemann Music Budapest in playing score size (235×310 mm).
The original edition contains the Critical Notes.

© 1999 for this edition by Könemann Music Budapest Kft.
H–1093 Budapest, Közraktár utca 10.

K 114&115&191/4012

Distributed worldwide by Könemann Verlagsgesellschaft mbH,
Bonner Str. 126. D–50968 Köln

Responsible co-editor: István Máriássy
Production: Detlev Schaper
Cover design: Peter Feierabend
Technical editor: Dezső Varga
Engraved by Kottamester Bt., Budapest

Printed by Dabas Printing House Co.
Printed in Hungary

ISBN 963 9155 83 7